The Saints

Volume 2

Text
Sr. Karen Cavanagh, CSJ

Cover Illustration
William Luberoff

Text Illustrations
Edward Letwenko

Regina Press
New York

Saint Thomas

was one of Jesus' closest friends. When Jesus rose from the dead Thomas said, ''I will not believe'' unless I touch Him. Jesus came again to see Thomas. Thomas told everyone about his love for Jesus, his friend.

July 3

My Prayer

Loving God, sometimes I wonder about you. Help me to trust in Your love even when I have doubts. Amen.

Saint Veronica

met Jesus as He carried His cross. It is told that
she wiped His face with her veil and that
Jesus left His image on her veil.

July 9

My Prayer
Let me see Your face in my friends and playmates,
O God, and let me help them when they are troubled.
Amen.

Saint Mary Magdalene

loved Jesus very much and followed Him to the cross. She stood with His mother and Saint John at the foot of the cross. She is the first person Jesus appeared to on Easter morning.

July 22

My Prayer
Loving God, I want to be loyal to you even in hard times. I want to be your follower. Please help me. Amen.

Saints Joachim and Anne

were the grandparents of Jesus and the father and mother of Mary, God's mother. They taught Mary her prayers when she was small and loved her very much.

July 26

My Prayer

Loving God, grandparents are very special people.
Please bless my grandparents and all grandparents for all the love they give to children. Amen.

Saint Martha

and her brother and sister, Lazarus and Mary, were very good friends of Jesus. He liked to visit their home and to talk with them about God.

July 29

My Prayer

Bless my home, dear God, and bless all the people who come to visit us. Help us to welcome them with kindness. Amen.

SAINT IGNATIUS LOYOLA

and his friends said that they would go anywhere in the world for God's glory. They called themselves ''Companions of Jesus'' (Jesuits) and today they are teachers and missionaries all over the world.

July 31

My Prayer

Loving God, help me to do the many good things that I do for you and let me be a good companion to my friends. Amen.

SAINT JOHN VIANNEY

was a parish priest in France. People came from all over the country to talk with him, to ask his advice, and to pray with him. He helped them come closer to God.

August 4

My Prayer

Loving God, I want to be close to you. Thank you for the people who help me and teach me to pray. Amen.

SAINT DOMINIC

wanted to preach God's message to the world.
He formed a group to help him do this.
He also had a special love for Our Blessed
Mother and gave the Church her
special prayer — the Rosary.

August 8

My Prayer
Mother Mary, help me to come closer to your son, Jesus,
and to listen carefully to God's message of love. Amen.

Saint Lawrence

said that the real riches in the Church are not the gold and silver but the poor and lonely people, the sick and saddened persons whom the Church helps. Lawrence spent his life helping them.

August 10

My Prayer

Loving God, help me to be generous and helpful each day. Help me to treat everyone with kindness. Amen.

SAINT CLARE

with the help of St. Francis of Assisi, began a group of sisters who live in silence each day so that they might think about God alone. They spent their lives living poorly and in prayer.

August 12

My Prayer

Let me take some time each day, dear God, to think of you and your love for me. Amen.

Saint Rose of Lima

cared for poor children, slaves, Indians, and elderly people who were ill, in her home in Peru. She is the first saint of the Americas and is the patron saint of South America.

August 23

My Prayer

God, give your special strength to those men and women in the world who care for and help the people who are the poorest. Amen.

SAINT MONICA

was a mother who tried to give her children the best education so that they would use their gifts for God. Her son Augustine turned from God's ways. She made her tears and sadness a prayer for his return to God.

August 27

My Prayer

God, sometimes I disappoint my parents and you. Help me to listen to them and to be loyal to you. Amen.

SAINT AUGUSTINE

turned back to God's ways and discovered
how wonderful God is. He wrote and
spoke of this goodness and his love
for God. He said that to stand
with God is to live forever.

August 28

My Prayer

Loving God, your ways are good and wonderful. I want
to tell of your love and to stand with you forever. Amen.

Saint Matthew

who wrote the first gospel, wasn't a popular person
in his town. Jesus chose him to be one of his
apostles. Jesus was letting us know that
everyone is welcome to God's
life and friendship.

September 21

My Prayer

God, you are a friend of everyone. Help me to be a good
friend all the time. Amen.

All Saints' Day

My Prayer

God, you call me to be a holy person. Your saints show
me how and your love gives me the strength. Keep me
close to you. Amen.

Saint Vincent de Paul

took care of the poor people in France. Men and
women helped him and today his followers
take care of sick people, orphaned
children, and elderly persons
all over the world.

September 27

My Prayer

Loving God, teach me to share what I have with people
who do not have as much and who need the help of
loving sisters and brothers. Amen.

Archangels — Michael, Gabriel, Raphael

Guardian Angels

The Bible tells us that God sent angels to guide and defend the people on earth. Jesus said that angels in heaven watch over and protect children on their way to God's Kingdom.

Archangels **September 29**
Guardian Angels **October 2**

My Prayer

Angels of God, be with me as I offer my prayers and praise to God. Protect me, too, as I work and play. Amen.

SAINT THERESE OF THE CHILD JESUS

was called the ''Little Flower'' because she did little things in a big way — the way of love.
She did everything as a gift for God.

October 1

My Prayer

God, you give me so many gifts. When I do good and loving things, I want them to be gifts for you. Amen.

Saint Francis of Assisi

loved God's people and all creation with a strong and gentle love. He built the first Christmas creche and that custom continues all over the Christian world today.

October 4

My Prayer

Loving God, help me to care for the world and all people with a strong and gentle love. Amen.

Saint Teresa of Avila

was always lively and loving. She had many friends and wrote books about her friendship and love for God. People who want to love God more, still read her books.

October 15

My Prayer

Loving God, you created me to be filled with life. Let my life be filled with love for you. Amen.

SAINT MARGARET MARY

loved God with all her heart. One day Jesus appeared to her and showed her His heart so filled with love for all people. Margaret spent her life telling people of Jesus' love for them.

October 17

My Prayer

God of love, keep my heart filled with your love and let me show your love to everyone. Amen.

Saint Luke

was one of the four writers of the gospels.
He also wrote about the early Christian
Church to whom Jesus sent the Holy
Spirit. Luke was a doctor.

October 18

My Prayer
Loving God, you are the one who makes people well.
Bless all doctors and nurses who care for sick people.
Amen.

Saint Isaac Jogues and Companions

wanted to teach the Indians in North America about God's love, even if it meant that they would die doing it. Isaac was killed by an Indian war party who didn't understand the way of God's love.

October 19

My Prayer

God, help me to find ways of telling others how much you love them. Amen.

SAINT MARTIN DE PORRES

studied medicine so he could care for the sick people.
He could only do this in the poor section of the city
where a black person would be welcome.
He joined the Dominican Order
in Lima, Peru where everyone
loved him.

November 3

My Prayer

God, help me to be aware when people need me and
never let me treat boys or girls differently because of
their color. Amen.

SAINT FRANCES XAVIER CABRINI

came from Italy to New York City and opened orphanages, schools, and a hospital. She always helped people who came new to this country and taught them about God.

November 13

My Prayer

Loving God, help me to always welcome newcomers, especially the new children in my classroom. Amen.

Saint Elizabeth of Hungary

was a queen who welcomed the people who were poor and sick into her palace. She cared for them as if they were her own children or family.

November 17

My Prayer
I want to see you, God, in all persons who are in need. Give me the eyes of your love. Amen.

SAINT CECILIA

wanted to spend her whole life in praise of God because she loved Jesus with all her heart. She is the patroness of music and musicians.

November 22

My Prayer

I love you, God, with all my heart. Let all my kind words and actions be like a song to you. Amen.

SAINT NICHOLAS

was a bishop who loved little children and told them about Jesus. Children believed that Nicholas would leave presents in their shoes or stockings in December.

December 6

My Prayer

God of love, let me think of your loving when I give or receive presents and wishes at Christmas time. Amen.

Saint John the Apostle

loved Jesus very much. He followed him faithfully
and stood under his cross on Calvary.
John wrote the fourth gospel,
the Gospel of Love.

December 27

My Prayer

I always want to be faithful to you, dear God. I want to
be with you and tell of your love by my life. Amen.

Draw your own picture showing how you would tell of God's love.

Write your own prayer to God:

____

____

____

____